Magna Carta in the Seventeenth Century

Maurice Ashley

Editor, The Listener
and B.B.C. Television Review

The University Press of Virginia
Charlottesville

© 1965 by the Rector and Visitors of
the University of Virginia

The University Press of Virginia
First published 1965

Library of Congress Catalog Card Number: 65-23456
Printed in the United States of America

FOREWORD

The aim of the following essay is to expound and summarize some of the work during the past fifty years or so on the history of Magna Carta in the seventeenth century. To those familiar with the subject my debt to Herbert Butterfield, *The Englishman and His History* (1944), J. G. A. Pocock, *The Ancient Constitution and the Feudal Law* (1957), and Faith Thompson, *Magna Carta: Its Role in the Making of the English Constitution* (1948), will be obvious. I am grateful to Mr. David Ogg, Mr. Ivan Roots, and Professor Austin Woolrych for suggesting sources to me, and to Mr. Roots for reading this essay in manuscript.

MAURICE ASHLEY

London, February, 1965

CONTENTS

3   Introduction

8   Bacon and Coke

13   The Reign of James I

17   Charles I and the Petition of Right

29   The Political Philosophy of the Charter

33   The Civil War

38   The Levellers

45   The Protectorate and Restoration

50   Exclusion and Revolution

55   Summary and Conclusion

Magna Carta in the
Seventeenth Century

INTRODUCTION

When that historic event at Runnymede, which we are again celebrating this year, was being commemorated fifty years ago, it was said by a distinguished scholar that there had in fact been two Great Charters: the original Magna Carta, conceded by King John to his barons in 1215, and the Charter as it was interpreted by the opponents or critics of the Stuart monarchy in seventeenth-century England.[1] Those critics—lawyers for the most part—had, it was felt, elevated or transformed what was in origin essentially a "feudal" or "medieval" constitu-

[1] W. S. McKechnie, "Magna Carta 1215-1915," in *Magna Carta Commemoration Essays,* ed. H. E. Malden (London, 1917), p. 12.

tional document into the palladium of English liberties.

Curiously enough, the very conception of a "feudal system" was invented in the seventeenth century, and it is to seventeenth-century historians and antiquarians that we should pay tribute as pioneers of English historical research into the early Middle Ages. Some of those historians, notably in the later half of the century, restored a sense of balance about the "feudal" nature of the original Charter, to which the lawyers, in their enthusiasm for the subject's rights, gave a rather fictitious background. Nevertheless it is to Sir Edward Coke, the celebrated advocate and judge, the father of what has been called "the Whig interpretation of English history," and to his contemporaries and friends that we are indebted for transmuting the Charter into a symbol of what most of us understand today by "political freedom."

Superlatives were then employed about it. In a famous paragraph in his *Second Institute* Coke wrote:

> As the goldfiner will not out of the dust, threds, or shreds of gold, let passe the least crum, in respect of the excellency of the metall: so ought not the learned reader to let passe any syllable of this law, in respect of the excellency of the matter.

Even before the seventeenth century, men like Robert Beale, the Elizabethan antiquary, and Sir James Morice, a Member of Parliament, declared that the Charter was "the law of laws," of such fundamental significance that royal letters patent could not touch it.[2] John Speed, writing in 1611, explained how King John had been

---

[2]Faith Thompson, *Magna Carta: Its Role in the Making of the English Constitution, 1300-1629* (Minneapolis, 1948), pp. 286-93 (hereinafter cited as Thompson, *Magna Carta*).

"constrained to grant . . . [the] uttermost desires" of his subjects and how thus "one of the greatest sovereigns of Christendom" had, in accepting Magna Carta, "become the twenty-sixth petty king in his own dominions."[3] Francis Ashley, a Reader in the Middle Temple, also taught in 1615 that if the Charter was a part of the common law of the land, it was indeed the law of laws. A pamphlet published in 1643 claimed that the law which the Great Charter embodied was "the highest inheritance the King hath." Sir Roger Twysden (1597-1672) thought he might "call it the foundation of our common law."[4] John Lilburne, the leader of the Levellers, in 1645 regarded it as the supreme charter of popular liberty.[5] Through the efforts of Coke, "the only genuine commentator on the Charter until modern times," the Great Charter was made "to walk again." In the words of Professor Herbert Butterfield, it "once again became a landmark in our history, because thinking made it so."[6]

The Great Charter that was usually discussed in the seventeenth century, however, was not King John's Charter of 1215 but the shorter version of the Charter promulgated in the name of John's son, King Henry III, ten years afterwards. This Charter was first published in 1499 and translated into English in 1534. But John's

[3]"Englands Monarchs," in *The Theatre of the Empire of Great Britaine* (London, 1611), p. 503.

[4]Roger Twysden, *Certain Considerations upon the Government of England,* ed. J. M. Kemble (London, 1849), p. 59.

[5]*Tracts on Liberty in the Puritan Revolution,* ed. William Haller (New York, 1934), I, 105.

[6]Herbert Butterfield, *The Englishman and His History* (Cambridge, 1944), p. 55 (hereinafter cited as Butterfield, *The Englishman*).

Charter was also known. Two copies of the original were presented to the antiquarian, Sir Robert Cotton, in the sixteen-twenties, though it was not in fact printed until 1759. The existence of John's Charter was familiar to Coke, and another lawyer, John Selden, printed a version of it given by the thirteenth-century chronicler Matthew Paris. *A Declaration of the Liberties of the English Nation,* published in 1681, observed that "Magna Carta and Charta de Foresta, being both made in 9 Henry III and confirmed Edward I do in effect treat of the same matter and therefore both are called the Great Charters of the Liberties of England."[7] This was typical of the frequently inaccurate ideas about the original Charter which prevailed in the seventeenth century. It was thought, for example, that the Charter was called "great," not because of its size, but because, as Coke wrote, "of the great importance and weightiness of the matter";[8] it was not accepted that it was first so called simply in order to distinguish it from the forest charter issued at the same time.[9] And it was usually referred to as "a statute," although Parliament—at any rate, Parliament as the seventeenth century knew it—did not come into being until years afterward.[10]

Because it was King Henry III's Charter of 1225 that was the subject of most of the comments and disquisitions by lawyers and statesmen, and because this was a shorter

[7] *Ibid.,* p. 27.

[8] *The Second Part of the Institutes of the Laws of England* (London, 1681), p. iv (hereinafter cited as Coke, *Second Institute*).

[9] W. L. Warren, *King John* (New York, 1961), p. 237n.

[10] Cf. M. A. Judson, *The Crisis of the Constitution, 1603-1645* (New Brunswick, 1949), pp. 80 ff.

charter than that of King John (it had only thirty-seven chapters or clauses as compared with sixty-three), the predominance of questions about the liberties or privileges of the King's tenants in chief, was perhaps less noticeable. In Henry III's Charter, wrote Professor Faith Thompson, "the binding force of the grant in perpetuity was strengthened by the declaration that any policy or enactment contrary to the terms of the Charter was to be held invalid." Thus "here in the text of the document itself was suggested the conception of the Great Charter as a sort of fundamental law...."[11] And it was possible for public men to concentrate their attention on the two or three chapters, notably 28, 29, and 30, which were considered to be particularly applicable to the political situation in the reigns of the first two Stuart kings.

To underline the value of this Charter, it was emphasized again and again that it was supported by six other "statutes" promulgated in the reign of King Edward III. Coke claimed that it had been confirmed over thirty times, and it is said to have been discussed in thirty Parliaments. Yet Magna Carta seems to have been largely forgotten or overlooked in Tudor times.[12] It was known to the chroniclers and lawyers, but it was sometimes referred to by writers as if it were mainly concerned with wardships, therefore of minor importance only. That curious document, *The Mirror of Justices,* wrongly believed in the seventeenth century (it was first published in 1642) to be a brilliant work on medieval law comparable with that of Bracton but in fact written

[11] *Magna Carta,* p. 383.
[12] *Ibid.,* pp. 216-30.

by a London fishmonger, asserted that Magna Carta's "forty points" had been "damnably disused." Professor Thompson has shown how some of the Elizabethan lawyers, who were in sympathy with the Puritans in their struggle against Archbishop Whitgift, quoted Magna Carta against him with fervour but not with much effect. "Magna Carta," observes Professor Butterfield, "did not save England from the despotism of the Tudors"– if despotism it was.[13] Queen Elizabeth I, after all, had understood when it was better to reprove, and when to yield concessions to, her faithful Commons. It was therefore not until King James I succeeded her on the throne and incautiously aired his provocative views about the divine right of kingship that Magna Carta was erected into "the cornerstone of English liberties," a charter not of the privileges of medieval barons and other social classes in the thirteenth century, but of the liberty of the English people as a whole, embodying a rule of law in which the most powerful or stubborn royal governments were expected to acquiesce.

BACON AND COKE

The two most famous lawyers of the reign of King James I were Sir Francis Bacon, who as Lord Chancellor was known as Lord St. Albans, and Sir Edward Coke, who was Chief Justice first of Common Pleas and then of the King's Bench until his dismissal by the King in 1616. Both, as behooved them in their positions, had a deferential regard for the laws of England. But Bacon's

[13] *The Englishman,* p. 29.

concept of the law was broader than that of Coke: he thought that three kinds of law—the common law, the statute law, and the law of nations (that is to say, received civil law)—made up the totality of the laws of England. Among other laws he attached importance to Magna Carta; he argued, for instance, that the governor of Bridewell, the famous house of correction in London, could not order idle ruffians to be seized and punished, as this was contrary to the Great Charter, which had been so often confirmed by statute—notably in 1368 by 42 Edward III, chapter 1, that said it was to "be holden and kept in all points; and if any statute be made to the contrary, that shall be holden for none."[14] But it is doubtful whether Bacon believed either that the Charter could never be altered again by any Parliament or that it could overrule the absolute powers customarily wielded by the monarch. Ideally Bacon believed that there could not possibly be any lack of harmony between the King's prerogatives and the subjects' rights since the King alone possessed the knowledge and intelligence to secure good government. When in 1612 the navy commissioners claimed the right to punish and imprison offenders against their regulations without reference to a court of law, Bacon maintained that this was completely legal, though later it was constantly argued that such action was entirely contrary to Magna Carta, just as the actions of the governors of Bridewell had been.[15] But the view

[14] Confirmation of the Great Charter, 1368, 42 Edw. III, c.1. See also Judson, *op. cit. supra* note 10, pp. 80-106.

[15] Samuel R. Gardiner, *History of England* (London, 1886), II, 187-99 (hereinafter cited as Gardiner, *History*). See *The Letters and the Life of Francis Bacon,* ed. James Spedding (London, 1868), IV, 346-57.

that Francis Bacon believed that the Great Charter established fixed and unalterable rules to which the government must always defer would appear to conflict with his basic political philosophy approving the wisdom of monarchy[16] and regarding even the judges as "lions under the throne."

That, on the contrary, was the concept of the Charter which Coke came to accept, although not apparently until after he had ceased to be a judge and had become a leading critic of the governments of James I and Charles I. Coke's famous commentary on the Charter in his *Second Institute* was not published until after his death, but his opinions are to be found scattered among his *Reports* and his speeches, particularly at the time of the debates in 1628 on the Petition of Right.[17] At one time Coke was much closer in his opinions to Bacon than he was to be later; he admitted at that earlier stage that Parliament could not tie the hands of its successors. As was pointed out during the debates in 1628, in 1615 he had signed a resolution of the King's Bench in which he approved of the doctrine that when the King's Council sent a man to prison the cause of the imprisonment need not be shown.[18] He had also in 1621 induced the House of Commons to abandon a scheme for an Act of Parlia-

---

[16]See Francis Bacon, *The Works*, ed. Basil Montagu (Philadelphia, 1842), II, 512. Charles Howard McIlwain, *The High Court of Parliament and Its Supremacy* (New Haven, 1910), p. 64, states that "even Bacon agrees with Coke that Magna Carta is unalterable." This view is refuted in J. W. Gough, *Fundamental Law in English Constitutional History* (Oxford, 1961), pp. 28-29.

[17]Thompson, *Magna Carta*, pp. 337-41, 354-74.

[18]Gardiner, *History*, VI, 243.

ment interpreting the twenty-ninth chapter of the Charter (chapter 39 of the 1215 Charter) in a manner which would have required bail to be granted to men imprisoned for matters of state.[19] But before he died in 1634, Coke's views were changed and more or less clarified. He said that they had been changed when the King ordered the arrest of Members of Parliament.[20] Magna Carta, he wrote, was supreme. It guaranteed private property and personal liberty even against the prerogative powers of the monarchy; not only statutes but judgments of the courts that ran contrary to it were invalid. The Charter was declared by him to be *"Charta libertatum Regni . . . quia liberos facit."*[21]

In his important book *The Ancient Constitution and the Feudal Law,* Dr. J. G. A. Pocock excellently summarizes Coke's final views on the Charter, which had two aspects:

In the first place he links the Charter, through Stephen Langton and Henry II, with the successive confirmations of the Confessor's law; and in the second he studies it clause by clause to prove that it enacts the main principles of common law and parliamentary liberty in his own day, so that the men of 1628 could believe that they were not only repeating the solemn act of 1215, but taking part in a recurrent drama of English history at least as old as the Conquest. The second process, by which Coke discovers the rights of parliament and property in a feudal document of the thirteenth century, was at bottom one with the greatest law so that precedents and prin-

---

[19]*Commons Debates 1621,* ed. W. Notestein, F. H. Relf, and H. Simpson (New Haven, 1935), IV, 308; Thompson, *Magna Carta,* p. 305.
[20]Gardiner, *History,* VI, 244.
[21]*Second Institute,* p. iv.

ciples laid down by the king's courts in the attempt to govern a feudal society could be used and found apt in the freeholding and mercantile England of James I.[22]

Still, as Professor Thompson pointed out, there was a certain inconsistency between Coke's emphasis on the Charter as fundamental law and the admission that it had been in fact modified and amended in the course of history.[23] In the end, however astute Coke might have been in his comments on certain clauses of the Charter, his interpretation of it was that of a political philosopher arguing that the Crown must always be completely subject to an ideal "common law" sharpened, moulded, and proved by experience rather than that of an advocate who could prove convincingly in the courts that the government might never act for the common good in an emergency by bypassing traditional procedures.

The clauses to which Coke and his disciples attached most importance in criticizing the policies of King James I were chapters 39, 40, and 41 of John's Charter, united into chapters 29 and 30 of that of Henry III. The 29th chapter was thus translated by Coke:

No freeman shall be taken, or imprisoned, or be disseised of his freehold or liberties, or free customs, or be outlawed, or exiled, or any otherwise destroyed; nor will we not pass upon him, nor condemn him, but by lawful judgment of his peers [*per legale judicium parium suorum*] or [*vel*] by the law of the land [*per legem terrae*]. We will sell to no man, we will not deny or defer to any man either justice or right.[24]

[22]Cambridge, 1957, p. 45 (hereinafter cited as Pocock, *Ancient Constitution*).

[23]*Magna Carta*, p. 360.

[24]*Second Institute*, pp. 45-57.

The chapter was interpreted as extending to villeins, except when they sought to invoke it against their own lord. *Per legem terrae* was taken to mean "by due process of law." The next chapter, the thirtieth, was interpreted to mean that all merchants were entitled to complete freedom in buying and selling.

It is needless to say that not all of these interpretations would satisfy scholars who have written meticulous glosses on King John's Charter. The translation of the word *vel* between *per legale judicium parium suorum* and *per legem terrae* has alone exercised many learned pens. The thirtieth chapter is generally held to have been intended to apply exclusively to alien merchants who had traded in England in the thirteenth century; it had nothing to do with general freedom of trade. But it did not matter that they were unhistorical interpretations; what has to be remembered is that these clauses were now coming to be used as effective arguments in the struggle between Parliament and the Crown for pre-eminence which dominated the history of England throughout the whole of the seventeenth century.

THE REIGN OF JAMES I

When King James I came to the throne of England, there was a growing consciousness that a change was about to take place in the shape of English history. The old Queen had kept her Parliaments in order, if sometimes with difficulty, and the House of Commons, though it had sometimes disliked her policies, was grateful for her leadership in the long war against Spain and had not pressed her too far or too hard. When James's first

House met in 1604, it was crowded and excited. It proved touchy about its privileges, which it soon claimed had been infringed by the new King. A recent American analyst has observed that "the house of 1604-1610 was more active and more self-assertive than its predecessors."[25] "Opposition members" began pressing their opinions, though as yet there was no formed opposition, any more than there had been in Queen Elizabeth's reign. The King, for his part, basing himself on his experiences in Scotland, had not expected such exuberance in Parliament and, when he first met it, tended to overstress his royal authority or prerogative powers.

The grievances ventilated by members of the Lower House were similar to those expressed in the previous reign: they related to their own privileges, to financial matters, and to ecclesiastical policies. The Great Charter had little bearing on the first question. But the Charter had spoken, if in no very clear terms, about two grievances still left over from much earlier times: purveyance and wardships. Purveyance was the right of the King's officers to requisition supplies and horses at a fixed price and was justified in the days when the Royal Court moved about the kingdom enforcing law and order. Now it was obsolete and oppressive. The Commons wanted purveyance and wardships to be abolished by the King and were even ready to grant him a small sum of money as compensation if he did so. Bacon told the King that since the times of Magna Carta his predecessors had made frequent laws against the excesses of purveyors. Both purveyance and wardships were men-

---

[25]William M. Mitchell, *The Rise of the Revolutionary Party in the English House of Commons, 1603-1629* (New York, 1957), p. 26.

tioned in the Charter, though by way of defining them rather than of reducing royal rights. It was, however, alleged in the Commons that the methods by which the purveyors enforced their rights ran contrary to the famous chapter 29 (chapter 39 of John's Charter).[26]

Another financial grievance arose out of the King's hitherto generally accepted power to regulate foreign commerce, as he regulated foreign affairs. John Bate was a merchant who had imported currants from the Levant and refused to pay additional customs or impositions levied by the Crown on his currants over and above the "tonnage and poundage" approved by Parliament. In this test case fought in 1606, the defence argued that such impositions were contrary to chapter 30 of Henry III's Charter (or chapter 41 of King John's) stating that "all merchants shall have safe conduct to go and come out of and into England" and be "free of illegal tolls." But it was difficult to stretch this chapter to cover the regulation of all foreign commerce; even "opposition" members of Parliament like William Hakewill accepted the judgment of the Court of Exchequer in the King's favour, although Coke in his later years insisted that the judgment was wrong. The King's ministers then proceeded to make use of the precedent established in Bate's case to extend the scope of impositions, which soon became a new grievance, especially among importers.[27] Impositions were violently attacked

[26]Robert Bowyer, *The Parliamentary Diary, 1606-1607,* ed. David Harris Willson (Minneapolis, 1931), p. 40. The Charter was aptly cited during the proceedings on the proposed union with Scotland. *Ibid.,* p. 219; Thompson, *Magna Carta,* pp. 247-48.

[27]*Select Statutes and Other Constitutional Documents,* ed. G. W. Prothero (Oxford, 1894), pp. 340-53.

during the last session of James's first Parliament, Sir Edwin Sandys claiming that they contravened chapter 30 of Henry's Charter, while Coke maintained that they were contrary both to John's Charter and the Charter as confirmed by Edward I. It has been suggested that Coke may have had chapters 12 and 14 of John's Charter in mind, that is to say, the chapters that have been held to mean that there could be no taxation of any sort without consent, though these chapters referred to scutages and aids, not to import duties, and were not specifically quoted by Coke.[28]

Another long-standing grievance in the Commons was monopolies and patents. Magna Carta had been quoted against them even in the reign of Queen Elizabeth I. Once again it was chapter 29 of Henry's Charter that was cited because it was argued that monopolists or patentees, in order to maintain their exclusive privileges, forcibly prevented men from carrying on their legitimate trades, thus depriving free men of their liberties. When in James's third Parliament a Bill was introduced into the Commons for "renewing" Magna Carta or "for the better securing of subjects from wrongful imprisonment and deprivation of trades and occupations contrary to the twenty-ninth chapter," it was aimed at monopolists like Sir Giles Mompesson, who was actually impeached with the King's approval.[29]

The Great Charter was referred to by opposition members in connection with religious questions, principally in relation to the jurisdiction of the ecclesiastical courts. Once again it was chapter 29 that was quoted.

[28]Thompson, *Magna Carta,* pp. 314-15.
[29]*Ibid.,* pp. 299-302; Gardiner, *History,* IV, 48-55.

The jurisdiction of these courts had long been a widespread grievance that grew even stronger in the reign of Charles I. The Court of High Commission, established in Queen Elizabeth I's reign, was a prerogative court that could imprison and fine offenders in ecclesiastical causes. The Puritans were bitter about it. Coke disliked it because its jurisdiction, in his view, lay outside the range of the common law. As Lord Chief Justice he frequently issued prohibitions against the High Commission and other courts to stop further proceedings until the common law courts had assured themselves that the matter at issue was indeed a spiritual one. Nicholas Fuller, a leading Puritan barrister, claimed that the powers of the High Commission were not only an infringement of chapter 29 but also of chapter 14—"a free man shall be amerced for a small fault only according to the measure thereof"—and of chapter 28—"in the future no bailiff shall upon his own unsupported accusation put any man to trial without producing credible witnesses to the truth of the accusation." Certainly to quote chapter 28 was a highly ingenious counter to the "ex-officio oath" which was imposed on accused persons by the Court of High Commission, requiring them in effect to testify against themselves.[30]

CHARLES I AND THE PETITION OF RIGHT

Thus by the time King Charles I succeeded his father on the throne the Great Charter was being quite frequently used both in Parliament and in the law courts to sustain

[30]Thompson, *Magna Carta,* pp. 256-62.

the doctrine that there could be no taxation without representation and no imprisonment of free men except by due process of law. Charles was a more stubborn character than his father, although he did not talk so much: at the crux James, like Elizabeth, had yielded to parliamentary pressure, though without admitting that his royal authority or prerogative power was in any way limited by law, for was not the monarch himself the fountain of all law? Charles inherited a big and expensive war with Spain and the services of his father's favourite, the first Duke of Buckingham, who waged war incompetently. Because his first Parliament disapproved of Buckingham's conduct of the war, it denied adequate supplies to the new King. Charles I was therefore driven to impose a forced loan on his subjects in 1626, and his Privy Council ordered the arrest and imprisonment of over seventy wealthy men who refused to pay it. Five knights thus committed to prison sued out a writ of habeas corpus so that they might be released on bail, to which the return was made that they were imprisoned "by the special command of the king." When he heard that answer, one of the knights, Sir Thomas Darnel, deferentially withdrew from the case. The defence attorneys of the other four knights cited chapter 29 of Henry's Charter, claiming that *per legem terrae* meant that men could not be imprisoned except by due process of law; they maintained that "by special mandate of the king" could not be so described.

The Attorney General, Sir Robert Heath, however, "was able to show that the argument from Magna Carta proved too much, for if the clause about imprisonment prevented imprisonment by the Council it would prevent imprisonment before trial; and yet criminals were always imprisoned before trial" under the common law. Heath also asserted defiantly that a Council warrant was indeed part of the "law of the land." He urged that there were ample precedents for the Privy Council's action and that the only recourse of the prisoners, if they sought bail, was to bring a petition of grace. After hearing the arguments, the Court of King's Bench decided that the knights were not entitled to bail, and they were remanded.[31] Before the next Parliament met, the King released all the prisoners who had refused to contribute to the forced loan. That was the end of the matter so far as the courts of law were concerned. But the King's action in introducing forced loans and imprisoning his subjects for refusing to pay them had aroused indignation among the Members of Parliament, notably Sir Edward Coke and the orator, Sir John Eliot. They were now determined that the rights of the subject, as defined by the Great Charter, must be reaffirmed by Charles I.

Sir John Eliot, one of the most outspoken critics of Charles I and his policies, had been among the rich men imprisoned for refusing to contribute to the loan.[32] Eighteen days before the Court of King's Bench had given its ruling in the case of the knights, Sir John had in fact sent a "humble petition" to the King. In it he insisted that he could not lend to the King without violating the liberties of the subject, since the loan was being enforced by imprisonment and restraint contrary to Magna Carta "by so many glorious and victorious kings

---

[31] J. R. Tanner, *English Constitutional Conflicts of the Seventeenth Century* (Cambridge, 1962), pp. 270-72.

[32] Harold Hulme, *The Life of Sir John Eliot* (New York, 1957), pp. 166-67.

so many times confirmed."³³ It is in connexion with Eliot's petition that we come across the first real note of scepticism in the seventeenth century about the historical validity of the Charter. Eliot had an old enemy in Sir James Bagg, the vice-admiral of South Cornwall and a toady of the Duke of Buckingham, who was the Lord High Admiral. In a letter to the Duke commenting on the terms of Eliot's petition, he argued that Magna Carta had been forcibly exacted both from King John and from his son, Henry III.

King John, having as cracked a title as Henry the first, had used the same policy in selling his regality. For, being environed with a rebellious army in the meadows of Staines, he was forced by a strong hand to grant the Magna Charta de Foresta [sic] . . . . Nor yet was the Magna Charta, thus extorted, a law, till the 52nd year of Henry the third. Neither was it then so freely enacted by royal assent . . . as wrung out by the long, bloody, and civil wars of those never-to-be-honoured barons! . . . It never was, as now, especially by a single brain, made a chain to bind the king from doing anything and a key to admit the vassal to everything!³⁴

But few Members of Parliament in the sixteen-twenties would have been found ready so to denigrate the Great Charter. As has been noted, a Bill for renewing the Charter had been introduced into the Commons in 1621 and read three times, though it did not reach the Lords; in the Parliament of 1624 a Magna Carta Bill was twice read. Again, the Charter was quoted in the impeachment charges framed against the Duke of Buck-

---

³³John Forster, *Sir John Eliot* (London, 1872), I, 413; Thompson, *Magna Carta,* p. 328.

³⁴Forster, *op. cit. supra* note 33, I, 414.

ingham in 1625, and it was cited once more when in May 1626 Eliot and Sir Dudley Digges were arrested by the King's orders for making insolent speeches in the House of Commons.[35]

Thus, when King Charles I's third Parliament met in March 1628 with the arguments in the five (or rather four) knights' case ringing in the members' ears, never before had the Charter been held in higher respect as the embodiment of a rule of law again and again violated by the King's ministers and officers with forced loans, martial law, and the billeting of his soldiers on civilians in the course of the wars. Charles I himself was not much concerned about all this. For he was now absorbed in a war not only with Spain but also with France; the Duke of Buckingham had been humiliatingly defeated in an attempt to relieve the town of La Rochelle held by French Protestants against Cardinal Richelieu; money was therefore urgently needed to continue the fight. In his opening speech on March 17, the King told Parliament that he had summoned it only because it was the speediest and best way to obtain supplies in a time of national danger; if it did not do its duty, he would have to proceed by other means. The Commons, led by Eliot, by Sir Thomas Wentworth, a hardheaded Yorkshireman, and by the aging Coke, were not to be intimidated and soon made it plain that they would vote no supplies until their grievances had been remedied.[36] "Projectors," said Wentworth—meaning the royal advisers—"extended the Prerogative of the King beyond the just symmetry which

[35] Hulme, *op. cit. supra* note 32, pp. 139-46.
[36] C. V. Wedgwood, *Thomas Wentworth* (London, 1961), pp. 61-75.

makes a harmony of the whole." Commons must therefore reinforce "the ancient laws made by our ancestors."[37] The spirit of the Great Charter brooded over all their deliberations.

The first concrete proposal to meet their aims put forward in the House of Commons was a Bill presented by Coke in which he wished to have imprisonment without cause shown declared clearly illegal. But the Bill was felt to be at once too complicated and not to go far enough. The Great Charter had included in its scope a wider field of English liberties. Eliot observed that the Charter and the many statutes confirming it had laid it down that "no subject should be burdened with any benevolences, loans, tasks, prises or such like charges."[38] Wentworth proposed to substitute a Bill of Rights invigorating and defining the old laws.[39] The debates that followed were long, complicated, and obscure. The King, who was in a pressing hurry to get money, sent frequent messages to Parliament urging it to let him have supplies but found difficulty in interrupting the flow of constitutional ideas. To stimulate his interest, he was promised on Good Friday a large sum represented by five subsidies. But after Easter the question stuck in the Commons, and on April 28 the King, striving to push them on, came to the House of Lords and told Parliament that he agreed that Magna Carta and its six attendant statutes were in full force, assured Parliament that he would maintain all his subjects in their justice,

[37] *Ibid.,* p. 63.

[38] See Cobbett, *Parliamentary History of England* (London, 1807), II, 275-76 (hereinafter cited as *Parliamentary History*). See also Thompson, *Magna Carta,* p. 336.

[39] See *Parliamentary History,* II, 278.

freedom, and the safety of their estates, and insisted that his royal word was as good as any law.

The leaders of the opposition in the Commons, however, felt that, though they might trust the monarch, they could not trust his ministers. Vainly Sir John Coke, the veteran Secretary of State, informed them that Charles I was the best of kings; vainly Sir Benjamin Rudyerd, a moderate royalist esteemed for his learning, declared:

> For my own part, I shall be very glad to see that good, old decrepit Law of Magna Charta which hath been so long kept in and lain bed-rid as it were; I shall be glad I say to see it walk abroad again, with new Vigour and Lustre, attended by the other Six Statutes: For, questionless, it will be a general heartening to all.[40]

But the terms on which the King was prepared to agree to a Bill were insufficiently heartening to Eliot, Wentworth, or Sir Edward Coke. For Charles I had made it perfectly plain in his speech that all he was willing to do was to accept the reaffirmation of the Charter in general terms; he would not agree to any detailed explanations about what it was now held to mean. Eliot demanded that they should have the whole Bill and nothing but the Bill. Next day Coke introduced what he believed was wanted: the first part of the Bill contained a restatement of Magna Carta; the second embodied resolutions of the Commons on imprisonment, taxation, and billeting. Imprisonment was the main grievance, and chapter 29 of Henry's Charter again came into play. But the King would have none of this at all. On May 1 the Commons were again told that the King would merely give his royal word, and their feelings were wounded

---

[40]*Ibid.*, pp. 335-36; Thompson, *Magna Carta,* pp. 335-47.

further when Sir John Coke made defiant observations about the right to commit a man to prison in the King's name. On May 5 King and Commons confronted one another. The Speaker told him that they still wanted their Bill of Rights; the King replied that he would only accept a Bill confirming the Great Charter "without additions, paraphrases, or explanations."[41]

It seemed as if an impasse had been reached, but next day on the initiative of Sir Edward Coke (taking up a suggestion put forward earlier by Dudley Digges) the Commons decided to introduce, instead of a Bill, a "petition of right," which adapted to public use a private procedure inviting the King to waive his prerogatives in favour of the normal course of law.[42] The Petition, which was read three times and finally accepted on May 26 by the House of Lords, asked the King "for recognition of a claim that every subject of the Crown had been wronged in certain specific matters and that, in future, the law would be observed."[43] Even that the King tried to evade. His first answer was the meaningless one that he would see that "right was done according to the laws and customs of the realm."[44] A conflict of

[41] *Parliamentary History*, II, 347. See generally Frances Helen Relf, *The Petition of Right* (Minneapolis, 1917); Gardiner, *History*, VI, 263-71; Butterfield, *The Englishman*, p. 68; E. R. Adair, "The Petition of Right," 5 *History*, n.s. 99 (1920).

[42] *Parliamentary History*, II, 349. Sir Edward Coke stated that "the King's answer is very gracious; but what is the law of the realm, that is the question. . . . Let us put up a Petition of Right: not that I distrust the King, but that I cannot take his trust but in a parliamentary way." *Ibid.*

[43] See *ibid.*, pp. 374-77.

[44] *Ibid.*, p. 377.

wills had come into the open between Charles I and his Parliament. The King threatened prorogation; the Commons made ready to impeach the Duke of Buckingham for treason. In the end the King yielded and said, "Soit droit fait comme il est desiré."[45] But whether even these words gave the Petition of Right the force of law was later to be disputed.

The Petition, thus accepted by Charles I on June 7, 1628, began by referring to the statute called "The Great Charter of the Liberties of England" and to other "good laws" which had earlier in history condemned the imprisonment of the King's subjects without cause shown and other contemporary grievances.[46] It also reminded the King that no man could be forejudged of life or limb against "the form of the Great Charter" and that "by the said Great Charter, and other laws and statutes of this your realm, no man ought to be adjudged to death, but by the laws established in this your realm, either by the customs of the same realm, or by acts of parliament."[47] But even the ultimate acquiescence of the monarch in these fine phrases did not assuage the wrath of the Commons or induce them to abandon their witch-hunt for the blood of the Duke of Buckingham. On June 26, to save Buckingham's life, the King prorogued Parliament.

Writing eighty years ago, S. R. Gardiner in his *History of England* compared the Petition of Right with the Great Charter thus:

---

[45]*Ibid.*, p. 409; Gardiner, *History*, VI, 309.
[46]*Parliamentary History*, II, 375-76.
[47]*Ibid.*

The Petition of Right has justly been deemed by constitutional historians as second in importance only to the Great Charter itself. It circumscribed the monarchy of Henry VIII and Elizabeth as the Great Charter circumscribed the monarchy of Henry II. Alike in the twelfth and in the sixteenth century the kingly power had been established on the ruins of an aristocracy bent upon the nullification of government in England. Alike in the thirteenth and in the seventeenth century, the kingly power was called to account as soon as it was used for other than national ends. Like the Great Charter, too, the Petition of Right was the beginning, not the end of a revolution.[48]

It is doubtful if the whole of Gardiner's argument would be acceptable to historians today. For example, it could plausibly be claimed that both Charles I and the leaders of the parliamentary opposition were striving, according to their lights, for what they regarded as "national ends." But Gardiner's last point is just. Most historians would agree that the importance of the Charter of 1215 lay not so much in what it achieved at the time as what it pointed to in the future.[49] In the debates on the Petition of Right the Charter was on everyone's lips. But its interpretation by the Crown and the Crown's servants still differed fundamentally from that of the authors of the Petition. The judges who had taken part in the five knights' case reiterated their view that the terms of Magna Carta did not prevent the King from committing men to prison without showing cause. Charles I himself, as late as May 12, had asserted that were his authority to imprison men when he thought fit to be taken away

[48]VI, 311.

[49]See A. E. Dick Howard, *Magna Carta: Text and Commentary* (Charlottesville, Va., 1964), pp. 22-23.

"the foundation and frame of the monarchy" would be "dissolved." Nor was he prepared to admit that he could not still levy tonnage and poundage—that is to say, customs duties—without the consent of Parliament. In proroguing Parliament on June 26, he said: "I owe an account of my actions to God alone." He reminded the two Houses that when the Petition was under discussion they had professed that it "was no ways to trench upon my prerogative.... [T]herefore it must needs be conceived, that I have granted no new, but only confirmed the ancient liberties of my subjects," and what those liberties were, he added, must be decided by the judges to whom only "under me, belongs the interpretation of the laws."[50] The King in fact imprisoned Members of Parliament again in that very year and asserted that his right to do so had not been changed by the Petition of Right.[51]

Thus indeed the importance of the Petition of Right, as of the Great Charter, lay in the historic future. It was a standard to fly in the civil wars. But it was not a pronouncement of general principles like the American Declaration of Independence or the French Declaration of the Rights of Man in later days. The Commons believed that they had induced the King to meet them over specific complaints; they had not yet in so many words laid down broad constitutional principles about men's liberty and the rights of property. For example, the old grievance of impositions had not even been mentioned in the Petition of Right; neither had tonnage and poundage. The Commons, when they met again in January 1629,

[50]*Parliamentary History*, II, 434.
[51]Gardiner, *History*, VI, 324-25.

after Buckingham had been assassinated, tried to argue that the Petition of Right covered tonnage and poundage, but they laid greater stress on the point that one of their own members had been imprisoned by the King for his failure to pay, and that this was a breach of privilege—a totally different issue from "no taxation without consent." Rather than give way over tonnage and poundage or accept criticisms of his religious policy, Charles I then dissolved his Parliament and governed his kingdom without one for eleven years. It is doubtful whether the Petition of Right made the slightest difference to his administration during those years. On the contrary, he exploited his prerogative powers to the full. He continued to raise tonnage and poundage; he introduced another tax, ship money, levied on inland towns as well as on ports, to pay for his navy, although the Petition of Right had said that "no man hereafter should be compelled . . . to yield any . . . tax . . . without common consent by act of parliament."[52]

Still the subjects of the King now had two "liberty documents," instead of one, to which they might appeal. When John Hampden refused as a point of principle to pay his share of ship money in 1637 and his case came before the Barons of the Exchequer, extensive use was made by his counsel of arguments deriving from the Great Charter, just as when in 1628 Hampden had also refused to contribute to the forced loan he had said he had feared to draw upon himself "that curse in Magna Charta which should be read twice a year against those that infringe it." But in the ship-money case (in which

[52]*Parliamentary History,* II, 376; *The Constitutional Documents of the Puritan Revolution,* ed. S. R. Gardiner (Oxford, 1906), p. 69.

Sir Edward Coke. (Courtesy of the Library of Congress)

The Petition of Right of 1628.

(Courtesy of the Public Record Office, London)

John Lilburne. (Courtesy of the British Information Services)

a majority of the judges found for the King) the King's counsel, Sir John Bankes, employed arguments not dissimilar from those used by Sir James Bagg when he commented to Buckingham on Eliot's petition and questioned the evidence of a particular text of the Great Charter, drawn up in King John's reign, because "it was an enforced act from a distressed king" and what John had been obliged to concede was alienable and could rightly be recalled by his successors.[53]

THE POLITICAL PHILOSOPHY OF THE CHARTER

In 1641, on the eve of the Great Civil War, Sir Edward Coke's heir, at the request of the House of Commons, agreed to the posthumous publication of his father's commentary on the Great Charter in his *Institutes*. Earlier King Charles I had prohibited publication, fearing it might be to the prejudice of the prerogative. By Coke and his followers the Charter was conceived to embody fundamental law or customary law stretching back to times out of mind in English history. Customary law, they thought, was more important than statute law because it had been tried and tested and approved and sanctified by time. Magna Carta, in Coke's view, contained principles which derived not merely from Edward the Confessor and Anglo-Saxons but even set forth the full law of King Arthur's days. The Normans had not deflected the course of English history. William I had

[53]Gardiner, *History*, VIII, 271-77; Tanner, *op. cit. supra* note 31, pp. 273-77; *Constitutional Documents*, supra note 52, pp. 108-24.

been no conqueror, for he had sworn to observe the ancient laws of the land, which he summarized in a Magna Carta, known as "the laws of King Edward." And even if the lawyers of the Norman kings had aimed at establishing absolutism or "sovereignty," that had been put right when the Angevins had accepted the Great Charters of John and Henry III. But even these Charters merely reaffirmed fundamental and immemorial customs. Henry I had promised to abandon the evil customs introduced by his two predecessors, and King Stephen and King Henry II had confirmed the laws of good King Edward in their coronation charters. Did not Matthew Paris say that the charters of King John contained little that was not to be found in the charters of Henry II and in the laws of Edward the Confessor?[54]

The laws of England were therefore older and more majestic than its monarchs, and by those laws all kings must abide. "Magna Charta," said Sir Thomas Wentworth, "is not acquainted with sovereign power." "Sovereign power," said Coke, "is no Parliamentary word; it weakens *Magna Charta,* and all our Statutes."[55] It has been wittily said of Coke," wrote Professor J. W. Allen,

that he invented Magna Carta: and certainly the version of it which he propagated was largely a fiction. Apparently he saw in it an expression of fundamental law of

---

[54]Pocock, *Ancient Constitution,* pp. 30-55. See Coke, *Second Institute,* pp. iv-ix. For the Commons' request to print Coke's commentary, see *The Journal of Sir Simonds D'Ewes,* ed. Wallace Notestein (New Haven, 1923), p. 358.

[55]John Rushworth, *Historical Collections* (London, 1703), I, 356.

the realm, not mutable, and a revival of principles that had been recognized in England since it was English.[56]

These principles included guaranties of the right of private property and of the freedom of the individual, above all from arbitrary imprisonment by the Crown. Magna Carta, so the majority in the House of Commons believed in the sixteen-twenties, secured subjects both from wrongful imprisonment and from the deprivation of their trades and occupations. All that had always been ensured by chapter 29. And Coke would have agreed with Francis Ashley, a lawyer but no Whiggish parliamentarian, when he taught that the "statute proclaimed liberty for the subject."[57]

The Charter, it was argued further, was not merely the foundation and embodiment of the immemorial common law of the land but also reaffirmed and provided for the regular holding of Parliaments. Antiquarians like Sir Henry Spelman and Selden discovered this from a study of chapter 14 of King John's Charter:

For obtaining the common counsel of the kingdom concerning the assessment of aids ... or of scutage, We will cause to be summoned, severally by Our letters, the archbishops, bishops, abbots, earls, and great barons; We will also cause to be summoned, generally, by Our sheriffs and bailiffs, all those who hold lands directly of Us, to meet on a fixed day ... and at a fixed place.

The *baro* or baron was interpreted by several antiquarians of the seventeenth century to mean all freeholders. Were not "the barons of London," John Wild-

[56] *English Political Thought, 1603-1660* (London, 1938), pp. 35 ff.

[57] Thompson, *Magna Carta,* pp. 284-93; *Puritanism and Liberty,* ed. A. S. P. Woodhouse (London, 1938), p. 371.

man, an attorney who delved into the past, argued, another name for the City's free men?[58] Thus not merely the common law but Parliament dated back at least to the time of the Charter.

Coke and his followers, like Eliot and John Pym, conceived the government of England to be "mixed." The monarch was merely the chief executive officer of the State; only the King in Parliament was supreme. The King out of Parliament was subject to many limitations; he was not "above the law," as a few extreme royalists claimed or were to claim later, but below the law. From the time of Bracton this fact had been stated by many political writers and speakers, though they had very different ideas of what they meant by "the law." To medievalists it usually meant the law of nature, the law of God, or the moral law, not the immemorial common law of Sir Edward Coke. But was the law itself sufficient to restrain the King from arbitrary government? Could he be forced to realize, as the celebrated American historian, Charles Howard McIlwain, once claimed, that Magna Carta was indeed "a fundamental law which binds a king and beyond which he may not go"?[59]

The early Stuart kings believed—and in this belief they were upheld again and again by the judges—that they possessed authority to go outside the common law and to disregard Parliament in times of foreign wars or national emergencies. It was on that basis that King

[58] John Wildman, *London's Liberties* (1651; 2d ed. 1682); Maurice Ashley, *John Wildman* (New Haven, 1947), pp. 73-76.

[59] *Op. cit. supra* note 16, p. 57. See Charles Howard McIlwain, "Magna Carta and Common Law," in *Magna Carta Commemoration Essays, supra* note 1, p. 122.

James I had levied impositions, that Charles I had exacted ship money, and that men had been arrested and imprisoned by royal warrant without cause shown. The King's ministers and supporters were prepared, with Francis Bacon, to argue that in normal times there could not possibly be any disharmony between the rule of law, the privileges of Parliament, and the authority of the King. Few royalists in the first half of the seventeenth century made absolutist claims in the modern sense of the term. Charles I had promised more than once that he would abide by Magna Carta, as he interpreted it.

In fact, when the Civil Wars came, when Parliament finally decided that it could no longer trust Charles I to recognize the logic of "mixed monarchy," subject to the laws, it was the parliamentarians who began to put forward absolutist claims, because they failed to see how the monarch could be constrained to obey the fundamental laws if he did not wish to do so. Did not Charles I as his very last action before leaving London in 1642 commit a breach of the letter and spirit of the Great Charter by attempting to arrest five Members of Parliament? Sanctions were therefore necessary. John's Charter had contained its own sanctions in setting up a committee of twenty-five barons to ensure that the Charter was fulfilled. Might not new sanctions now be required? And were not those who had the right to impose those sanctions in fact the ultimate sovereigns?

THE CIVIL WAR

When the Long Parliament met in November 1640, King Charles I was obliged to make many concessions to its constitutional demands, if only because he had been defeated in his wars against the Scots. But in the end the Civil War broke out since the majority in the House of Commons distrusted the King and were not prepared to put into his hands the control of the militia or of the army needed to suppress a rebellion in Ireland. The theoretical reasons adduced for the change of attitude toward the monarchy were many and were often inconsistent. It was claimed that the King's ministers had given him bad advice and that the Earl of Strafford, in particular, had violated the fundamentals of the Constitution. Men like John Pym and Oliver Cromwell were not really theoreticians; their eyes fixed on hard political realities, they sought specific reforms in Church and State. But numerous pamphleteers were ready to present a plausible case for broad constitutional changes after the Civil War began.[60]

Some of these political pamphleteers—Philip Hunton is a notable example—emphasized that England was a "mixed monarchy" and that it was one of the fundamentals of the Constitution that the two Houses of Parliament should have a share in sovereignty. (In his *Treatise of Monarchie* [1643] he said that Magna Carta had permanently limited royal power.) The royalist writers did not repudiate the concept of mixed monarchy. Indeed, the Reverend Henry Ferne, one of the most respected of royalist pamphleteers, fully admitted it; so did Sir John Spelman, the son of Sir Henry, the famous antiquarian. In the answer which the King himself gave to the nineteen propositions presented to

[60] Allen, *op. cit. supra* note 56; *Chapters in Western Civilization,* ed. Contemporary Civilization Staff of Columbia College (New York, 1961), I, 447.

him by Parliament on the eve of the Civil War, he also accepted this concept.[61] But to make the King into a mere figurehead, as the parliamentary demands seemed to propose, was, the royalists retorted, to destroy, not sustain, the fundamentals of the Constitution.

Thus it came about that other parliamentarian apologists began to move away from the idea of mixed monarchy and even from stressing the value of such unalterable laws as the Great Charter. Charles Herle, a Lancashire clergyman, who was to take a prominent part in the Puritan Westminster Assembly, while he still stuck to the doctrine of mixed monarchy, wrote in his *Contra-Replicant* (1642) that "nothing had done us more harm of late than this opinion of adhering to law only for our preservation." For if the King could break the fundamental law, where was there security? Henry Parker went farther. He claimed that Charles had forfeited his rights because of his bad government; he had overridden the law: "[T]was not difficult to invent laws for the limiting of the supreme governors but to invent how those laws should be executed or by whom interpreted was almost impossible." Power was needed to uphold the law, and the responsible classes represented in Parliament were the right people to do it. Thus they could in good conscience take up arms against the King.[62]

William Prynne, perhaps the most influential of all the parliamentary pamphleteers of this epoch and himself a lawyer and antiquarian, was even more outspoken about the protection afforded by such fundamental laws

[61]*Chapters in Western Civilization,* I, 447.

[62]P. 45; Henry Parker, *Observations upon Some of His Majesties Late Answers and Expresses,* in *Tracts on Liberty, supra* note 5, II, 167-213.

as the Charter. To him Magna Carta had been the triumph of reactionary clergy.[63] He agreed with Henry Parker that it had been "penned by Popish bishops"; he equated Stephen Langton, one of the supposed authors of the Charter, with a later Archbishop of Canterbury, William Laud, whom the Long Parliament was to send to the scaffold for treason; and he disagreed with Herle that the barons' resistance to the tyranny of King John was noble. Ought not Charles I, like King John, to be rescued from clerical intrigue? "But," writes William Lamont, "Prynne's loss of faith in the monarch's good intentions . . . only strengthened his scepticism of the value of Magna Carta."[64] Magna Carta was no effective guaranty against a bad King: such fundamental laws were weak assurances. Thus Prynne, like Parker, distrusted paper guaranties and maintained that logically the right constitutional solution was to accept the sovereignty of Parliament, "the sole law-maker, and having an absolute sovereignty over the laws themselves (yea, over Magna Carta and all other objected acts)...."[65] "Parliament," he said in his *Sovereign Powers of Parliaments and Kingdoms* (1643), was "above all laws, statutes, yea Magna Charta." The royalists professed to be shocked and even invoked Magna Carta on their own side. But Prynne was never a consistent writer, and one can quote passages from his writings in praise of the Charter as securing the liberties of Englishmen. Prynne even used

[63] William M. Lamont, *Marginal Prynne* (London, 1963), pp. 93-97; William Prynne, *The Sovereign Power of Parliaments and King James* (London, 1643), II, 39.

[64] Prynne, *op. cit. supra* note 63, II, 96.

[65] *Ibid.*, p. 97.

the history of the Charter as a precedent for calling in foreign aid against a tyrannous king, as the Scots were called in during 1644.

In such historical arguments Prynne could claim the support, not merely of Parker, but of other antiquarians. Sir Henry Spelman indeed by his general view of "feudalism" had cast doubt on Coke's interpretation of the Charter as the embodiment of fundamental law. Still the fact remains that most of these pamphleteers used the Charter to sustain their own political conceptions or misconceptions. Some of them envisaged it as typifying the rule of law that the King had broken; some as demonstrating the dangers of popish conspiracies; others even considered it a proof of the importance of Parliament since time out of mind. In 1643 a pamphlet about the Bridewell case, first discussed by Bacon, was printed. This was used to show that it was "by the Law that both the King and all the subjects are ruled and directed," and the pamphlet was entitled *Brief Collections Out of Magna Carta* or *The Known Good Old Laws of England*.[66] But one would search with difficulty the reports of the debates of the Long Parliament for any references to the Charter. The fact is, as the writings of Parker, Herle, and Prynne indicated, that the political argument was moving to another plane. The concept of "mixed monarchy" was falling into disrepute among parliamentarians disillusioned with Charles I and Coke's beloved "fundamental law"; the Great Charter was now widely believed to be no real protection against determined attempts at royal absolutism.

[66] B.M., E 38(12).

THE LEVELLERS

While parliamentarian pamphleteers, such as Herle, Parker, and Prynne, were beginning to argue that the liberty of the individual subject could better be protected by the sovereignty of Parliament than by any paper guaranties, however ancient and historic, another vigorous group of political propagandists, who came to be nicknamed the "Levellers," began to insist on the value of the fundamental law enshrined in Magna Carta as their rightful shield against the tyranny of Parliament itself after Parliament had defeated Charles I in the First Civil War. The leader of this new movement was John Lilburne, who had arrived in London from the north as a clothmaker's apprentice when he was fourteen and in 1638 had been ordered by the Star Chamber, the royal prerogative court, to be whipped at the cart's tail from the Fleet prison to Westminster for distributing pamphlets against the bishops. For this exploit he became known as "Freeborn John." He enlisted and fought as an officer on the parliamentarian side in the Civil War; he believed, as he afterward stated, that it was "on behalf of the laws . . . above all for Magna Carta and the Petition of Right that the Parliament took up arms."[67] Soon taken a prisoner, he was exchanged by the royalists, fought under Oliver Cromwell in East Anglia, and served as a lieutenant colonel at the battle

[67] *A Discourse betwixt John Lilburne, Close Prisoner in the Tower of London, and Mr. Hugh Peters, upon May 25, 1649*, in H. N. Brailsford, *The Levellers and the English Revolution* (Stanford, Calif., 1961), p. 553, 579n.1.

of Marston Moor (1644) in the Earl of Manchester's regiment of dragoons. Cromwell afterward accused Manchester of being a slothful commander, and Lilburne backed him up. He refused to subscribe to the Covenant, which committed the English to a Presbyterian state religion, and therefore resigned from the army and devoted himself to political agitation. In July 1645 Lilburne was arrested by orders of a committee of the House of Commons for slandering the Speaker. It was then that he first quoted Magna Carta (chapter 29) in his own defense.

Summoned before the Committee of Examinations, Lilburne demanded to know the reason for his commitment. "I build upon the Grand Charter of England," he claimed; "I have as true a right to all the priviledges that doe belong to a freeman, as the greatest man in England." The Great Charter, he asserted, was his "birth-right."[68] Charles I's ministers, Strafford and Laud, had lost their heads because they "trod Magna Carta under their feet."[69] When removed from the presence of the committee, Lilburne insisted on reading the Charter to the serjeant-at-arms. The next time he appeared before the committee, he was accompanied by a crowd of sympathizers who demanded justice according to Magna Carta. Nevertheless he was committed to Newgate prison.[70] While he was in Newgate, a petition in his favour was presented to the House of Commons, and he himself published a pamphlet outlining his

[68]*Copy of a Letter . . . to a friend,* in Pauline Gregg, *Free-born John* (London, 1961), pp. 120, 376n.30.

[69]*Ibid.,* p. 16, in Gregg, *Free-born John,* pp. 121, 376n.32.

[70]Gregg, *op. cit. supra* note 68, pp. 120-22.

troubles entitled *England's Birth-Right Justified,* in which he fastened on Magna Carta as the supreme charter of popular liberty. Finally, in October, the House of Commons released him, having in fact laid no charge against him. But his experiences damped Lilburne's ardour for Parliament and drew him toward the conclusion that a written constitution was necessary to protect the industrious classes of the nation, like himself, against the gentry in Parliament as well as against a tyrannical monarchy.

Another distinguished Leveller thinker associated with the mercantile classes was William Walwyn, an older man than Lilburne, who has been called the Plato of the movement. Walwyn exerted himself to help Lilburne in his prison days. But he was very doubtful of the wisdom of using the Great Charter as the first line of defence. In his pamphlet, *Englands Lamentable Slaverie* (1645), which he addressed to Lilburne, Walwyn wrote that Magna Carta

is but a part of the people's rights and liberties, being no more but what with much striving and fighting, was by the blood of our Ancestors, wrestled out of the paws of those Kings, who by force had conquered the Nation, changed the laws and by strong hand held them in bondage.

For though Magna Charta be so little as less could not be granted with any pretence of freedom, yet as if our Kings had repented them of that little, they always strove to make it less, wherein very many times they had the unnatural assistance of Parliaments to help them.[71]

Thus Parliament had failed to enlarge the bounds of "that deceitfully and improperly called Magna Charta,"

[71] In *Tracts on Liberty, supra* note 5, III, 313-14.

which had been so abridged as to become "a very blotted book." One should not therefore call out for Magna Carta "like great Diana of the Ephesians . . . calling that mess of pottage the birthright, the great inheritance of the people, the Great Charter of England."[72] Magna Carta, he thought, "hath been more precious in your esteem than it deserves," for the people still remained under intolerable oppressions which could only be put right by Parliament. Ultimate reliance must be placed on "open and universal justice" and on the judgment of the good people of England.[73]

It was evident that Lilburne was shaken by his friend's argument, for in *The Just Mans Justification,* which he published in 1646, he agreed that Magna Carta was "but little" and observed that although it was commonly thought to be the Englishman's inheritance, it fell far short of "the Saxon laws" and was merely the best that could be extorted by force from a despot.[74] Another Leveller, Richard Overton, writing about the same date, said flatly: "Magna Carta itself being but a beggarly thing, containing many marks of intolerable bondage, and the laws that have been made since by Parliaments, have in very many particulars made our Government much more oppressive and intolerable."[75] Overton thought it was Parliament's duty to establish their liberties and not to rely on the Charter; Walwyn wanted a new charter to be drawn up instead of trying to patch the old one.

[72]*Ibid.,* p. 314.
[73]*Ibid.,* p. 315.
[74]Perez Zagorin, *A History of Political Thought in the English Revolution* (London, 1954), p. 11.
[75]*A Remonstrance,* in *Tracts on Liberty, supra* note 5, III, 365.

Thus the Levellers themselves began to put forward constitutional documents such as their Agreement of the People of 1647 and their Large Petition of 1648. The Agreement, as Professor Woodhouse pointed out, accepted "the notion of inalienable rights embodied in Magna Carta."[76]

In spite of the doubts thus cast upon the extreme claims for the Charter by the Levellers who, in contradiction to Coke, thought that William the Conqueror had indeed destroyed English liberties and the good old Saxon laws and placed them all under a yoke that must be shaken off, Lilburne continued to quote the Charter in his own personal defence. In June 1646 he had again been committed to prison, this time by the remnant of the House of Lords for insulting one of their members, and during the next two years he had to direct his propaganda activities from a cell in the Tower of London. When he was first arrested he insisted fiercely that the Lords had "trampled Magna Charta under foot" and he would as soon draw his sword against them as he had done against the King. "Magna Charta," he claimed, "hath justly, rationally, and well provided that your Lordships shall not sit in judgment or passe sentence in Criminall causes, upon any Commoner of England either for life, limbe, liberty, or estate."[77] But even when General Fairfax's army, having quarrelled with the Presbyterian-directed House of Commons, advanced on London in August 1647 in order to "purge" Parliament, and Fairfax himself entered the Tower and called for Magna Carta, declaring that "this is what we have fought

---

[76] *Puritanism and Liberty,* supra note 57, p. 71.
[77] Gregg, *op. cit. supra* note 68, p. 139.

for . . . and must maintain," Lilburne was still left there to languish.⁷⁸ For a short time he was allowed out of the Tower at the end of 1647, but he promptly took part with his friend and fellow Leveller, John Wildman, in a demonstration in the City and was soon back in the Tower as a close prisoner. Before their commitment Lilburne and Wildman engaged in reading together Coke's commentary on the Charter, hoping to persuade the House of Commons of the illegality of their arrest. They impressed the soldiers guarding the House with their lore and eloquence, but not the Commons itself. They stayed in prison until August 1648. Then they were released and took part in discussions aiming to draw up their own charter of freedom or written constitution. But before this could be completed the King was tried and executed, and an oligarchic republic was set up at Westminster and Whitehall.

Lilburne and Wildman argued that both at Westminster and in the City of London, which had backed the parliamentarians against the royalists, a new system of government ought now to be introduced. They advocated a wider suffrage, but this, it is now thought, was not intended to be genuinely democratic, rather merely to extend the vote to persons like themselves who did not necessarily own a forty-shilling freehold, the lowest existing qualification.⁷⁹ They also wanted to restrain Parliament from infringing individual liberties by introducing a new, unalterable, fundamental law, more far-reaching than the feudal charter. In urging some degree

---

⁷⁸*Ibid.*, p. 190.

⁷⁹C. B. MacPherson, *The Political Theory of Possessive Individualism* (Oxford, 1962), pp. 107-59.

of democratization in the City government both Lilburne and Wildman mentioned the Charter, though Wildman explained in his tortuous language that while barristers might argue (with Coke) that any Act of Parliament contrary to the Charter was "null of itself" he himself believed that "right reason (*recta ratio*)" was the only sure principle to follow and alone should shape the common law of England.[80]

The new rulers—or at any rate the military section of them—though willing enough, as later events proved, to provide England with a written constitution laying down fundamental rights (as in the Instrument of Government and the Petition and Advice when Oliver Cromwell became Lord Protector) were not ready in the confused state of affairs that followed Charles I's execution in 1649 to tolerate the subversion of the victorious parliamentarian army by extreme Leveller doctrines. Vainly an attempt was made to persuade John Lilburne that the new rulers of England were good men and that if England were in future governed by God's Chosen People there would be no need for either a Magna Carta or a Petition of Right. Twice—in 1649 and 1652—Lilburne was arrested, tried, and acquitted, so popular was this firebrand hero of freedom in the City of London. Each time he appealed to the continuing validity of the Great Charter to save him from incarceration or death. But in the end he was forced into exile, intrigued with the royalists, and died a Quaker. Yet in spite of all his misfortunes he always clung to Magna Carta as the guaranty of his legal rights, though he admitted, with his

[80]Wildman, *op. cit. supra* note 58. See generally Ashley, *op. cit. supra* note 58, pp. 231, 298; *Puritanism and Liberty, supra* note 57, p. 371.

fellow Levellers, that "where Reason ceaseth, the law ceaseth."

THE PROTECTORATE AND RESTORATION

Although its authority on some points was occasionally questioned, the great principles attributed to Magna Carta by Coke and reflected in the Petition of Right were largely accepted in the second half of the seventeenth century. If, when Charles II was restored in 1660, both he and his Lord Chancellor, the Earl of Clarendon, revived the claims of the Stuarts to exercise fully the King's "regal and inherent power and prerogative," in fact Charles II behaved as a constitutional or at least semiconstitutional monarch.[81] The two main principles detected in the Charter—that taxation could not be imposed without parliamentary consent and that no subject should be imprisoned or put on trial except by due process of law—were, on the whole, followed by Charles II's government. It is true that neither Oliver Cromwell as Lord Protector nor James II, Charles's successor, obeyed the latter principle. When Cromwell, before his first Parliament met, claimed to levy customs duties by ordinance under the Instrument of Government, a merchant named George Cony refused (in 1654) to pay, his counsel claiming that the demand was a violation of Magna Carta. The Chief Justice, Henry Rolle, evidently agreed, for he resigned rather than determine the question. Other justices who expressed qualms were dismissed, and Cony's lawyers were sent to the Tower

[81]David Ogg, *England in the Reign of Charles II* (Oxford, 1934), II, 450-60.

of London. Cony withdrew his plea, and his lawyers apologized. Cromwell thus took a strong line. "The people," he asserted when Parliament met, "will prefer their safety to their passions, and their real security to forms, when necessity calls for supplies." Other judges began talking about Magna Carta: Clarendon (a very poor authority) relates that the Lord Protector made rude remarks about the Charter. Like the early Stuart kings, Cromwell maintained that the executive had the right to employ emergency powers in times of national crisis. Although he allowed that Parliament had the right to impose or confirm the imposition of taxes, and although he tried to govern according to the law, he realized the practical limitations of Coke's theories, especially after a revolution.[82]

James II, like Cromwell, also collected customs and excise duties in the first months of his rule without the consent of Parliament; but again, as in Cromwell's case, Parliament confirmed the need to collect such duties. As to imprisoning men without showing cause, Cromwell proved in Cony's case that he was capable of doing so. Charles II and James II, on the whole, refrained from that, though men like Sir James Harrington and John Wildman were sent to the Channel Islands where writs of habeas corpus did not run. No Member of Parliament was put into prison for words spoken in the House

[82] Charles Firth, *Oliver Cromwell* (New York, 1908), p. 418; Edward, Earl of Clarendon, *The History of the Rebellion,* ed. W. Dunn Macray (Oxford, 1888), VI, 93. Both Lord Morley and John Buchan accepted this story, Morley saying, "[T]he Protector scoffed at Magna Charta with a mock too coarse for modern manners." John Morley, *Oliver Cromwell* (New York, 1900), p. 387. It is strange how many biographers of Cromwell swallow any story about him, however doubtful the source.

MAGNA CARTA IN THE 17TH CENTURY

of Commons, as had happened in the times of Elizabeth I and Charles I, but James II's House sent one of its own members to the Tower for insulting the King. The Habeas Corpus Amendment Act of 1679, forced through in the dying days of Charles II's third Parliament, against the wishes of the executive, in fact made it harder than before for the Crown to send men to prison and keep them in prison without showing cause. James II regarded the Act as a definite obstruction to the royal authority and would have liked to get it repealed. Subsequently it proved necessary to suspend the Act in times of national crisis. It proved to be a more effective protection of the rights of the subject than the Great Charter ever was, even if it in fact reflected the principles of the Charter's twenty-ninth chapter as interpreted by Coke.

Charles II's second Parliament, which sat for eighteen years, inevitably changed in character before it was dissolved. But it was very historically minded, and precedents from the distant past were often quoted with relish during its debates. For example, when Charles II dismissed the Earl of Clarendon from office, making him the scapegoat for the failure of a war against the Dutch, the Commons attempted to impeach him for treason before the Lords. The Lords refused to commit him on the grounds that no particular act of treason had been assigned against him. "They insisted," complained John Vaughan, afterward Lord Chief Justice of Common Pleas, "much upon Magna Charta, which saith that no man shall be condemned or tried but by his peers and the laws of England, nor shall any man be imprisoned but by due process of law." Vaughan himself asserted that there were "divers cases in which a man may be imprisoned which are not with the Great Charter," for example, "the Crown or prerogative law, which differs from common proceedings." More persuasively, perhaps, he added that Parliament itself had the power to imprison its own members without due process of law.[83] The Commons were probably too angry with the Lords to question these arguments. But meanwhile Clarendon himself had withdrawn abroad, and the two Houses agreed upon an Act of Banishment. William Prynne, a member of this Parliament, and, as has been seen, a man with a tempered admiration for the Charter, nevertheless claimed that it was against the Charter to banish Clarendon without his having ever been heard at the Bar.[84]

In this same session the Commons summoned Sir John Keeling, Lord Chief Justice of the King's Bench, to its Bar to answer various accusations that had been made about his conduct of cases brought before him. He was said to have slighted Magna Carta and therefore "should be speedily brought to his answer." Specifically it was asserted that when a prisoner brought before him had claimed the privileges of Magna Carta he had called it "Magna Farta"[85] (this was the phrase that Clarendon had attributed to Cromwell) and asked, "What ado with this hath we?" The Lord Chief Justice explained to the House of Commons that

As to the slight speaking of Magna Charta, he affirmed that it being long since he did not remember, nor believe that he said those words, yet he was not absolutely cer-

[83] John Milward, *The Diary,* ed. Caroline Robbins (Cambridge, 1938), p. 150.

[84] *Debates of the House of Commons,* ed. Anchitell Grey (London, 1763), I, 65 (hereinafter cited as *Debates of Commons*).

[85] Milward, *op. cit. supra* note 83, p. 163.

tain that he did not speak them, but it might be possible, Magna Charta being often and ignorantly pressed upon him, that he did utter that indecent expression, but as he doth not remember, neither can it reasonably be imagined that he should speak these words in any dishonour of the Great Charter...."[86]

After the Chief Justice had withdrawn, the Commons debated his case for four hours and in the end voted that "in the pleas of judicate he hath undervalued, vilified, and condemned Magna Charta, the great preserver of our freedom and property," but they decided not to proceed further against him.[87]

The Great Charter was mentioned in two other famous constitutional cases in Charles II's reign, *Skinner v. East India Company* (1668) and *Shirley v. Fagg* (1675). Skinner brought a grievance about the seizure of one of his ships by the East India Company before the King in Council and was referred to the House of Lords. It was felt in the Commons that it was improper to take a common plea direct to the Lords; such procedure, it was claimed, was entirely contrary to chapter 29 of the Charter, for it was neither to submit to due process of law nor to judgment by one's equals. The result in the end was that the House of Lords did not again try to act as a court of original jurisdiction.[88] In the other case, Fagg was a member of the House of Commons who was so injudicious as to attend the House of Lords when Dr. Shirley brought a suit against him there on appeal from the Court of Chancery. The in-

[86]*Ibid.*, p. 167.
[87]*Ibid.*, p. 170; *Debates of Commons*, I, 67.
[88]*Debates of Commons*, I, 451.

dignant Commons sent him and his lawyers to the Tower. Each House quoted the Charter on its side; the Lords maintained that the Commons were interfering with the due process of law when they imprisoned members of their own House for appearing at the Lords' Bar. In this case the Commons finally lost the argument; the appellate jurisdiction of the House of Lords was henceforward accepted even where members of the Lower House were concerned.[89]

EXCLUSION AND REVOLUTION

After the first or Long Parliament of Charles II's reign was dissolved in 1679, a movement to exclude James, Duke of York, from the succession to the throne on the ground that he was known to be a Roman Catholic reached its peak of virulence and passion. Three "exclusionist parliaments" met, two at Westminster and one in Oxford. To preserve his brother's rights, Charles II dissolved all three of them and never held another Parliament in spite of the existence of an act requiring Parliaments to be held every three years. The result was that the question of the constitutional importance of the regular meeting of Parliaments was widely raised, and, curiously enough, the Great Charter was called as a witness for the longevity of Parliaments. We have seen how, earlier in the century, both Selden and Spelman had maintained that chapter 14 of John's Charter provided for the calling of a Parliament, though Spelman himself had recognized that kings were older than Parliaments.

[89] *Ibid.*, III, 239.

Medieval history was ransacked to produce arguments on this matter. Probably the majority of educated men then believed that Parliament dated back to the days of Alfred the Great. Certainly it was not doubted that Parliaments had met regularly in the thirteenth century. William Petyt, a barrister of the Inner Temple who was also an antiquarian of repute, maintained in his book *The Ancient Right of the Commons of England Asserted* (1680) that he could prove from the records that the Commons of England had been an essential part of Parliament before the forty-ninth year of Henry III's reign. The General Council that met at Runnymede, he observed, was called "Parliamentum de Runemed," and the title of baron applied to all freeholders.[90]

The same argument was sustained by William Atwood, a friend and pupil of Petyt. In his *Jus Anglorum ab antiquo* (1681) Atwood said that Edward I had confirmed Henry III's Charter and that Henry III had confirmed the Charter of King John. Therefore since John's Charter, chapter 14, had provided for the calling of a Parliament, it was obvious that Parliament must have been in existence at least since the time of Henry III. Moreover, it could be deduced from this same chapter 14 that there were two kinds of barons summoned to Parliament, the tenants in chief and others, and that these others were in fact the knights, citizens, and burgesses who filled the House of Commons in the seventeenth century.

The principal answer to Petyt and Atwood was provided by Robert Brady, a physician by training who as Master of Caius College, Cambridge, had elected to

[90] Pp. 33, 110.

turn himself into a historian in the royalist interest. (Whether it is helpful to describe Petyt and Atwood as Whigs and Brady as a Tory may be open to question.) Brady had carefully studied the writings of Spelman; he was convinced that William I had been a genuine conqueror and that there was a world of difference between the common and the feudal law. He was an exceptionally able controversialist "baffling and banging" his enemies and "chasing them like squirrels from tree to tree"; in his essay entitled "Jani Anglorum facies antiqua," part of a larger book, he laid about Atwood pretty effectively. He argued that the Common Council mentioned in John's Charter was simply the General Council of the kingdom and that its membership consisted purely of the tenants *in capite* and not, as Petyt argued, the counts, barons, clergy, and free men of all the kingdom. Henry III's Charter, he maintained, also referred only to an assembly of magnates of the realm and not to a modern Parliament, and King John's Charter and King Henry III's were identical. Brady was caustic about the Charter; it was a clerical document, he thought: "[T]he liberties, which our ancient historians tell were so mightily contended for, if seriously considered, were mainly the liberties of Holy Church, by which, in most things, she pretended to be free from subjection to a temporal prince."[91]

In his epistle to the reader in this book—its general title was an *Introduction to the Old English History* (1684)—Brady spoke of "two sorts of turbulent men who under plausible pretences have appeared for the

---

[91]*An Introduction to the Old English History* (1684), pp. 166-69, 175, 210; Pocock, *Ancient Constitution*, pp. 182-228.

Liberty of the People or indeed the Change of the Government"; there were those who preached that the origin of all power and government is from them, which was platonic and utopian, and those who "hold forth to the people ancient rights and privileges found in records, histories, and charters" and pretended that the word *baro* applied to the whole people. The object of these "ridiculous and ill-founded insinuations" was an "endeavour to undermine the government."[92] Brady, it can be said, was the first writer to attack the "Whig interpretation of English history," invented by Sir Edward Coke, by means of an effective inductive method of reasoning.

Another royalist writer had earlier attacked the Great Charter from a rather different angle. This was Sir Robert Filmer, whose books had mostly been written during the Civil Wars but whose *magnum opus, Patriarcha,* was not published until 1680, long after his death, when it helped to revivify the royalist cause. Filmer believed that from the time of Adam and Eve the monarch had always been the father of his people and was the author, interpreter, and corrector of the common law. "The statute of Magna Charta," he explained, "hath and must be understood of the institution then made of the ordinary jurisdiction in common causes, and not for restraint of the absolute authority which serves in rare and singular cases."[93] Magna Carta, he averred, had been exacted from the kings of England. "The Great Charter," Filmer added, quoting a sentence which he wrongly attributed to Sir Walter Raleigh, "had first an obscure birth

[92] Brady, *op. cit. supra* note 91.
[93] *Patriarcha and Other Political Works,* ed. Peter Laslett (Oxford, 1949), p. 110.

by usurpation, and was secondly fostered and showed to the world by rebellion."[94]

Several replies were written to this posthumous work of Filmer; among others were ones by James Tyrrell, Algernon Sidney, and John Locke. Sidney's reply was also posthumously published. On Magna Carta Sidney argued as follows:

> I agree with our author that "Magna Charta was not made to restrain absolute authority". . . . it was to assert the native and original liberties of our nation by the consession of the king then being, that neither he nor his successors should any way encroach upon them.[95]

Thus kings are kings only by law, and they might do nothing except what was given them by the law.

Although Sidney's enormous work replying to Filmer was not published until the reign of William III, the manuscript was found when Sidney himself was arrested and put on trial for treason at the time of the so-called Rye House plot in 1683. The manuscript was in fact used in place of the second witness required in a trial for treason, and its wicked republican tone was thought sufficient to send Sidney to his death on the scaffold. It has been suggested that it was understandable in view of this frightening precedent that no other replies were made at the time to the works of Filmer and Brady. Later Locke was to refute Filmer and put forward his own theories of government, theories far less dependent upon early history, in his *Two Treatises of Government*.

[94]*Ibid.*, p. 117; cf. Christopher Hill, *Intellectual Origins of the English Revolution* (Oxford, 1965), p. 212.

[95]*Discourse concerning Government* (Edinburgh, 1750), II, 234.

But even Locke refused to acknowledge his authorship, thinking perhaps of the ghost of Sidney on the scaffold.[96] Locke's book was also largely written in the time of the exclusionist agitation but was not published until after the Glorious Revolution of 1688. To pursue that story would take us far beyond Magna Carta. But it seems true to say that in spite of Spelman, Parker, Filmer, Brady, and others, many of the statesmen and political leaders of the last twelve years of the seventeenth century were convinced that the revolution which brought William III to the throne of England in place of the Roman Catholic James II had also restored the constitution to its historic and pristine principles of mixed monarchy founded on ancient English law. They believed, in the words of Professor Butterfield, that they had "made their conception of Magna Carta come true."[97] Some of them also believed that it was now time to produce another Magna Carta—and this was to be the Bill of Rights of 1689.

SUMMARY AND CONCLUSION

"No man," wrote Thomas Hobbes, most realistic of political philosophers, in his *Behemoth* (1679), "can have in his mind a conception of the future, for the future is not yet. But of our conceptions of the past, we make a future."[98] Modern historians of the seventeenth

[96]Ed. Peter Laslett (Cambridge, 1960), pp. 4-6.

[97]*The Englishman,* p. 78.

[98]Christopher Hill, *Puritanism and Revolution* (London, 1958), p. 55.

century have emphasized that many of the leading critics of the executive, at any rate during the first thirty years of the century, were engaged in conjuring up a totally fictitious picture of the past in order to establish a different outlook for the future. Sir Edward Coke, donning the robe of a constitutional lawyer and historian, invoked the clauses of a medieval charter, which he transformed into a fundamental and unalterable "statute" so that it should be a powerful warning to kings that they must not violate the personal liberty or menace the private property of their subjects; they must always accept the rule of law and pay deference to the High Court of Parliament. Medieval documents, including John's Charter, as described by Matthew Paris, Henry III's Charter of 1225, attended by the six "sister statutes" of Edward III's reign, the thirty-two confirmations of the Charter described by Coke, the *Modus tenendi Parliamentum,* the *De tallagio non concedendo, The Mirror of Justices,* and other records of varying authenticity, were all called upon as witnesses that the kings of England had confirmed limitations on their own powers and had recognized rights of their subjects that might never be infringed.

Although Coke and his followers were undoubtedly mistaken in some of the historical precedents to which they laid claim, it can be argued that they did not in fact misrepresent the spirit of the past as much as has sometimes been contended. It is true that Magna Carta was a document that emerged after a rebellion (just as in the reign of King John's son the Provisions of Oxford were exacted by force), that it was obtained by negotiation with an Archbishop of Canterbury and a group of barons, and that it was afterward repudiated, in part at least, by John's successors. It may also be accepted that it was not as full or extreme an expression of constitutional principles as was later asserted. On the other hand, it is now no longer thought to have been "the programme of a pack of feudal reactionaries."[99] And though it was not a revolutionary document at the time and merely expressed what the barons conceived to be the law, it did aim to protect the King's subjects from oppression and to achieve reasonable reforms in the light of experience. Modern historians would therefore be inclined to admit that the Charter, in however shadowy a way, did in fact envisage a rule of law and affirm the principle that consent was required for the imposition of extraordinary taxation. And though it is obvious that Parliaments in the seventeenth-century sense did not meet in the early thirteenth century, a clerk writing in 1244 did actually speak of the Parliament at Runnymede, while gatherings at which the King wore his crown and held parley with his greater subjects met with increasing frequency as the thirteenth century advanced.

The English people have always been averse to laying down broad theoretical principles of government, and the famous constitutional documents of the seventeenth century—the Petition of Right, the Bill of Rights, and the Act of Settlement—dealt with particular grievances against the Crown that it was felt needed remedying rather than with broader concepts hard to interpret. Even such pronouncements as the Apology of the House of Commons of 1604 and the Grand Remonstrance of 1641 partook of this rather practical character. The virtue of the Great Charter in the seventeenth century

[99]H. G. Richardson and G. O. Sayles, *The Governance of Medieval England* (Edinburgh, 1963), p. 388.

was that two wide principles were detected in it—that no man could be imprisoned except by due process of law and that no taxation could be levied except by common consent—principles hallowed by a glorious past, by historical precedents stretching back at least to Anglo-Saxon times and possibly to immemorial times. It could point a lesson and adorn a tale. These general principles were embodied in the Petition of Right, but Charles I was most reluctant to accept them in concrete terms. So fundamental law lent an air of sanctity to men who were in fact becoming revolutionaries. The Civil Wars were won and lost. The restoration of the Stuarts followed. But men never completely forgot the Great Charter. And when James II was forced to flee from London in 1688, the two Houses of Parliament, summoned as a convention by Prince William, were able to agree that the fundamental laws had indeed been broken and that a new charter was needed to put matters right. But at the same time it was believed, as all good royalists wished to believe, that the Revolution had restored the ancient law of the land.

The parliamentarians who fought the Civil War and executed Charles I forty years before the Glorious Revolution also were convinced, at least at the outset, that they were restoring an ancient constitutional fabric and making triumphant Coke's conception of the common law enshrined in the Great Charter. But doubt came increasingly to be felt about the viability of the Charter. John's Charter had an inbuilt arrangement for its enforcement, and during the reign of Henry III an active baronial opposition was able to ensure that the royal charters should be kept. Yet here was a basic difficulty that advocates of the principles of the Charter were reluctant to recognize: if the King did not keep his promises, there was no means of making him do so except in the last resort by the threat of civil war. If civil war were needed whenever the King's government violated constitutional principles, that would mean that the nation was liable to be in a constant state of anarchy. That was what worried Thomas Hobbes and was the reason why in his *Leviathan,* written during the Civil Wars, he could admit no restraint upon the powers of the executive. And that was why other writers, notably those who supported the parliamentarian cause, were inclined to argue that the idea of "mixed monarchy," in which the executive was balanced by Parliament and controlled by a rule of law, had become harder and harder to sustain.

Thus though up to the eve of the Civil War men such as John Pym still paid lip service to the concept of mixed monarchy and the virtues of fundamental laws like the Great Charter and the Petition of Right, the wars in the end were fought not so much for the continuation or preservation of the laws as in order that people might be freed from them. At least that is what the Levellers came to believe. Astute soldier-politicians like Henry Ireton and John Lambert, who helped to win the victory over the King, therefore put forward schemes for fresh written constitutions, though these too could only be enforced by the rule of the sword. Hugh Peter, one of Oliver Cromwell's chaplains, appears to have been quite frank in admitting that it was no longer possible to live under the shadow of the past. "It is very advisable," he said, "to burn all the old Records, even those in the Tower," for they were "the monuments of tyranny." He tried to persuade John Lilburne, the Leveller leader, that "good men, not good laws, must save kingdoms" and that once the Chosen People of God governed they would "have no need for Magna Carta or the Petition of Right. Coke and Littleton would vanish, with all the other relics of heathenism, popery and tyranny."[100]

Subsequently, it seems, the argument advanced on two levels. On the one hand, there were those who continued to believe that Magna Carta and the Petition of Right were signposts along a road that has been called the "common-law account of history." "It was still perfectly possible," Dr. Pocock writes, "to see the Revolution in terms of the 'myth of confirmations,' ranking 1688 and 1066, 1215 and 1628 in the list of dates on which the ancient and fundamental law had been solemnly reasserted by the nation."[101] Both in the works of political philosophers or pamphleteers and in the debates of the two Houses of Parliament much use was still made of legal and historical precedents for the affirmation of political rights. When the Revolution came, William Petyt, who had taken the Great Charter to be evidence for the longevity of Parliament, was appointed Keeper of the Records in the Tower of London in place of Robert Brady, the iconoclast, and was responsible for associating the legitimization of the change of government with the doctrine of the immemorial constitution in which the Charter played so large a part.[102]

Yet, on the other hand, the real makers of the Revolution—men like Danby, Shrewsbury, and Bishop Comp-

[100] See Hill, *op. cit. supra* note 98, pp. 77-78.
[101] *Ancient Constitution,* p. 232.
[102] *Ibid.,* pp. 229-54.

ton—were mostly political realists, and John Locke, the philosopher of the Revolution, though he invented an imaginary state of nature, set little store by genuine historical argument. Filmer, the Tory apologist for absolutism, had been the chief provider of historical (and religious) arguments in the reign of Charles II and required refutation, but the new Whig philosophy of Locke was not dependent on Sir Edward Coke. In fact, philosophers or political theorists during the seventeenth century tended to sanctify revolutions after they had happened. Parker and Herle justified the Civil War after it started; John Milton justified the execution of King Charles I and the establishment of the Cromwellian republic after the events. If John Locke wrote his *Two Treatises of Government* before the Revolution of 1688, it was because he was justifying the policy of the Whigs or exclusionists who ten years earlier claimed that the succession could and should be altered and thus performed a dress rehearsal for Prince William of Orange's invasion.

All this is not to say that by the end of the century the Great Charter had ceased to be revered or thought of as a symbol of a Golden Age. The idea that Englishmen were free and equal in Anglo-Saxon times and even elected their rulers continued to be taught by historians as late as the nineteenth century, when the Charter was described by so notable a constitutional historian as William Stubbs as the "first great public act of the nation after it had realized its own identity." In more recent times we have come to acknowledge the significant role fulfilled by historiography in the lives of the nations, since men struggling for their freedom can be consoled by the thought that all they are seeking is a reversion to the pattern of the good old days. That is what converted Magna Carta into a "liberty document" so important in the seventeenth-century history both of England and the English colonies across the Atlantic, including those which were to become the United States of America.

Augsburg College
George Sverdrup Library
Minneapolis, Minnesota 55404

JN
191
A8

77754